Just a few months into _____ decreeing "A New B_____ tionship between Islar_____ Obama took pains to ch_____ for the occasion of his auspicious speech. He picked al-Azhar University in Cairo.

Islam is beholden neither to synods nor to any formal ecclesiastical hierarchy. This ancient seat of Sunni scholarship is thus as close as it gets to a Muslim Vatican for Sunnis, vastly the majority sect among the creed's 1.4 billion adherents worldwide. Given that Islam also abides no metaphorical wall of separation between the spiritual and secular realms, it is unsurprising that al-Azhar's scholastic specialty is sharia. In Conrad Black's recent and apt description, sharia is Islam's "totalitarian legal system" for organizing society, "directed by clerics and going far beyond what even the most pious and fervent Westerner would consider the province of religion."

Translated as "the path," sharia is the corpus of Allah's law, prescribing a comprehensive legal and political framework. Though it certainly has spiritual elements, Black is correct that it would be a mistake to think of it as a "religious" code in the Western sense. It would control every aspect of life – from the sacred to the mundane, from veneration of the divine to worldly politics, economics, military operations, social relations, familial obligations, inheritance, and even gritty details of personal hygiene.

It is sharia, not terrorism, that must be our line of demarcation, dividing radical Islam (or, as it is variously known, "Islamism" or "political Islam") from moderate Islam. That is the thesis of a recent study called *Shariah: The Threat to America – An Exercise in Competitive Analysis.* I am one of the study's several authors. The group – featuring a wealth of national security experience drawn from the spheres of intelligence, law enforcement, the military, academe, and journalism – dubbed itself "Team B-II."

The name is an homage to the original "Team B." More than a generation ago, that array of skeptics took issue with détente – the

It is sharia, not terrorism, that must be our line of demarcation, dividing radical Islam from moderate Islam.

regnant early '70s view that the world was plenty big enough for both sides of the Iron Curtain to coexist and even cooperate in countless areas of mutual interest. That Team B profoundly influenced a certain California governor who would go on, as president, to defeat the Evil Empire and win the Cold War. Its conclusion was straightforward yet, at the time, bracing: The Soviet Union was wedded to a totalitarian ideology, Communism, that sought global hegemony and would relentlessly work – by means violent and nonviolent – to secure the defeat of the United States and its allies in order to obtain it.

Team B-II analogously concludes that there is today a global Islamist movement just as determined as were the Soviets to achieve worldwide dominion and as fully committed to use all means at its disposal – not just terrorism, not by a long shot – to destroy America and the West. By myopically focusing on jihadist violence, today's equivalents of the détente solons repeat their predecessors' perilous minimization of the threat to our way of life.

Preponderant in what Angelo Codevilla calls the "ruling class" (opinion elites in government, the academe, and the media), these purveyors of conventional wisdom insist that we need only concern ourselves with a fringe handful of "violent extremists." (It is no longer de rigueur to call them "jihadists" or even "terrorists" – since "terror" is inconveniently invoked in Islamic scripture, its mention in this Orwellian construct is deemed defamatory of Muslims.) The exertions of these said extremists have nothing to do with Islam. Indeed, the story goes, they constitute "un-Islamic activity" simply by dint of their being violent. Better to see their "root causes" as poverty, Western imperialism, cartoons, Guantanamo Bay, Israel, Abu Ghraib, or whatever hobby horse strikes bien-pensant fancy that particular week – it being a boon for progressives to cast their every bête noire as a catalyst of terror.

Team B-II surmises that this narrative is not only wrong but dangerously so. It is wrong because violent jihadists are actually catalyzed by an interpretation of Islam that, however heinous it may seem to us in the West, is entirely mainstream, firmly rooted in Muslim scripture, and favored by influential Islamic commentators, institutions, and academic centers – not least the faculty at al-Azhar. It is dangerous because although terrorism is the most obvious and horrifying means of pursuing radical Islam's hegemonic aspirations, it is neither the most prevalent nor the most effective.

To appreciate this, it is necessary to grasp what jihad is. There is, of course, raging debate between Islam's apologists and detractors over the concept's meaning. The former – including, significantly, President Obama's top counter-terrorism advisers – posit the revisionist fantasy that jihad is a peaceful, internal struggle for personal betterment. To the contrary, centuries of scholarship and tradition, including the four major schools of Islamic thought, hold that the genesis of jihad – in the Koran, the hagiographic biographical accounts of Islam's warrior-prophet, and the history of Islamic conquest – is strictly military. Bernard Lewis, the West's docent extraordinaire of Islam, has repeatedly acknowledged as much. Indeed, the encyclopedic *Dictionary of Islam*, first published by the British missionary Thomas Patrick Hughes in 1886, matter-of-factly defines jihad as "a religious war with those who are unbelievers in the mission of Muhammad." "No stronger retrograde force exists in the world," wrote Winston Churchill about Islam, reasoning that "far from being moribund, Mohammedanism is a militant and proselytising faith."

Let's put aside these uncongenial facts and indulge the smiley-face jihad preferred by the apologists. Though framed as a struggle to become a better *person*, it is actually the struggle to become a better, more faithful *Muslim*. That is a very different thing – not to improve in some cosmic sense but to conform one's life to the edicts of Allah's law, to sharia.

Trapped in the Western progressive's hedonistic infatuation with personal fulfillment, today's opinion elites miss the essence of Islam. It is a corporatist doctrine, determined to control the individual's life down to its granular details not for his sake but for the flourishing of the *ummah*, the notional Islamic Nation. In fact, as Islamists beguile Western intellectuals with odes to "freedom" and "democracy," it is critical to remember that Islam and the West proceed from different assumptions. The Islamic concept of freedom is nearly the opposite of ours, connoting perfect submission to Allah. When Islamists laud freedom, *that* is what they mean. The late Sayyid Qutb, radical Islam's most consequential modern theorist, stated the matter this way: "Islam began by freeing the human conscience from servitude to anyone *except Allah*, and from submission to any *save Him*." (Emphasis added.) Similarly, when Islamists praise democracy, they refer not to a culture of governance for self-determining people but to a potential means of imposing sharia by popular vote.

In Islamist ideology, the ummah thrives when the state enforces sharia, the perfect,

---

The Islamic concept of freedom is nearly the opposite of ours, connoting perfect submission to Allah.

---

immutable system personally bequeathed by Allah for the government of all creation. Understood this way, the apologists are quite correct in maintaining that jihad need not involve improvised explosive devices and hijacked jumbo jets. Whether pursued by forcible or nonforcible methods, jihad is always and everywhere the mission to implement, spread, and defend the advance of sharia.

Why should the West be concerned about this? The brute fact is that those who support sharia and its objectives, including the eventual establishment of a global caliphate, are perforce supporting goals that are incompatible with the United States Constitution, the civil rights it guarantees, and the representative government it authorizes to effect the will of a free people. Sharia rejects fundamental premises of American society and governance:

· *The bedrock proposition that the governed have a right to make law for themselves irrespective of any theocratic code.* In Islam, sharia is nonnegotiable and people are not at liberty to enact law that contradicts its terms.

· *The republican democracy governed by the Constitution.* In Islam, the Muslim ruler is obliged to govern in accordance with Allah's will, manifested by sharia.

- *Freedom of conscience.* In Islam, apostasy – either the renunciation of Islam or sowing treasonous discord within the ummah – is the gravest offense, punishable by death.

- *Individual liberty, including in matters of personal privacy and sexual preference.* In Islam, homosexuality and adultery are capital offenses, and other transgressions of sharia's prescriptions for social intercourse are brutally punished.

- *Freedom of speech, including the liberty to analyze and criticize theocratic codes and practices.* In Islam, blasphemy is deemed to include any form of expression that casts Islam or its prophet in an unfavorable light, and it results in savage retaliation.

- *Economic liberty, including private property.* While Islam vouchsafes private ownership, all property is deemed to belong to Allah and to be held in trust for the ummah by the nominal owner, who is thus beholden to the Islamic state regarding its use.

· *Equality.* In Islam, law is dramatically skewed to favor men over women, who are treated as chattel; it similarly advantages Muslims over non-Muslims, who are regarded as dhimmis, decidedly second-class citizens whose choice is to convert, pay a tax for the privilege of living in the Islamic state, or die.

· *Freedom from cruel and unusual punishments.* Islam's archaic huddud penalties include stoning, decapitation, the severing of limbs, etc.

· *An unequivocal condemnation of terrorism.* In Islamist ideology, barbarous attacks are rationalized as legitimate "resistance" whenever Islam is deemed to be under attack – particularly when non-Muslim forces occupy Islamic territory, even if those forces believe they are doing humanitarian work. (In Islam, efforts to plant Western ideas and institutions in Muslim countries are seen as attacks on Islam and violations of sharia.)

· *An abiding commitment to resolve political controversies by the ordinary mechanisms of federalism and democracy.* In Islamist ideology, Muslims are encouraged to use whatever political, legal, and other nonviolent means are available for advancing the cause of sharia, but when those avenues are ineffective, the use of force becomes obligatory.

Sharia, not terrorism, must be our bright line because it reliably divides Muslims who embrace the West from Muslims determined to Islamize the West. This sorting is essential because the vast majority of the latter are not terrorists. In fact, many of them actually condemn terrorism, though these condemnations tend to be dodgy: apt to rebuke "terrorism" in the abstract, but not specific terrorists, because in truth the attackers are seen as engaged in legitimate resistance and their victims as oppressors, not innocents.

Yet, taking these condemnations at face value, the salient point is that the dispute between nonviolent Islamists and jihadist terrorists is over methodology. Both camps wholeheartedly agree that Muslims are obliged to confront and subdue non-Muslims until every nation adopts sharia. The difference is that the terrorists regard the failure to impose sharia as an affront that must be bludgeoned into submission, while nonviolent Islamists follow a patient, sophisticated strategy that would incrementally impose sharia by marching through a society's institutions.

Islamists, violent and nonviolent, are in unison on sharia. On the other hand, sharia usefully divides Islamists from authentic Muslim moderates. True moderate and reformist Muslims embrace the Enlightenment's veneration of reason and, in particular, its separation of the spiritual and secular realms. For them, sharia is a reference point for a Muslim's personal conduct, not a corpus to be imposed on the life of a pluralistic society. By contrast, Islamists are Muslim supremacists, totalitarians who – just like Communists and Fascists – would impose their preferred regime, in this case a global theocracy. For them, sharia is not a private matter but an immutable, compulsory system that Muslims are obliged to install and the world required to adopt. Therefore, the West is an obstacle to be overcome, not a culture and civilization to be embraced, or at least tolerated. It is impossible, they maintain, for alternative legal systems and forms of government peacefully to coexist with the end state they seek.

We must no longer allow those who mean to destroy our society to camouflage themselves as "moderates." The definition of *moderation* needs to be reset to bore in on the sharia fault line. Only by smoking out those Muslims who wish to impose sharia can we succeed in marginalizing them. The true nature of the sharia system is such that anyone obliged actually to defend the proposition that it should be adopted in our country will find few takers. Sharia defenders will be seen for what they are in the West: fringe, extremist figures.

If President Obama's purpose in Cairo was to continue his courtship of America's detractors, he could hardly have chosen a better location than al-Azhar. Founded in the 10th century, the university's modern graduates are a who's who of jihadist grandees. The late Abdullah Azzam, for example, was one of al Qaeda's founders. Another alum, Omar Abdel Rahman, the infamous "Blind Sheikh," bragged about providing the Islamic approval (or *fatwa*) for the 1981 murder of Egyptian President Anwar al-Sadat and now serves a life sentence for leading the terrorist cell that bombed the World Trade Center in 1993. In fact, from his American prison cell, Abdel Rahman has been credited by Osama bin Laden for issuing the fatwa that approved the 9/11 atrocities.

At al-Azhar, such figures are far from aberrations. The institution's recently deceased

---

We must no longer allow those who mean to destroy our society to camouflage themselves as "moderates."

---

grand sheikh, Muhammad Sayyid Tantawi, construed Muslim jurisprudence to support suicide bombings. "Martyrdom" is similarly endorsed by the most influential living al-Azhar alumnus, Sheikh Yusuf Qaradawi, host of a weekly Al Jazeera television program, *Sharia and Life*, and trailblazer of the *Islam Online* website. Both of these media gambits are hugely popular in Muslim countries and, increasingly, in the West.

In fact, Qaradawi is now a trustee at Oxford University's Centre for Islamic Studies. Neither his endorsement of suicide terror against Israel nor his 2004 fatwa calling for the killing of American personnel in Iraq seems to have fazed the academy: In Europe and America, the sheikh is hailed as a "moderate" and a "reformer." And when Qaradawi received some bad publicity in the West for this fatwa against American troops, prominent members of the al-Azhar faculty instantly rallied to his defense – reflecting the consensus that Allah's law was profoundly offended by the sowing of

Western notions and institutions in Islamic countries.

Besides the fatwas, the media ventures, and his fomenting of the murderous global rioting by Muslims in 2005 over a Dutch newspaper's cartoon depictions of the prophet Muhammad, Qaradawi is best known for his role as spiritual adviser to the Muslim Brotherhood. Established in the 1920s by the Egyptian academic Hassan al-Banna, whose Salafist ideology urged a return to the unadulterated principles of Islam's founders, the Brotherhood (or Ikhwan) is Islam's most significant mass movement.

It now operates in dozens of countries. Some Ikhwan entities are unabashed terrorist groups. Hamas, for example, is the Brotherhood's Palestinian branch, and the financial, political, and moral support of its terrorist war against Israel has been a top Ikhwan priority for two decades. Nevertheless, most Brotherhood satellites do not engage directly in violence, though they are coy about supporting it – again, claiming to condemn "terrorism" while applauding "resistance." They present themselves instead as advocacy organizations, campaigning for "human rights," "civil rights," and "social justice." In essence, such campaigns are always and everywhere about the promotion of sharia. For the Brotherhood, Muslims are divinely enjoined to Islamize society – whether by violence, rhetorical persuasion, or stealth – and sharia's implementation is the necessary precondition for that end result. Thus the Brotherhood's motto, unchanged from its founding to this very day: "Allah is our objective. The Prophet is our leader. The Koran is our law. Jihad is our way. Dying in the way of Allah is our highest hope. *Allahu Akbar!* [Allah is the greatest!]"

The Brotherhood considers itself to be engaged in a "civilizational jihad" against the West. Its primary partner in that endeavor – since the late 1940s, when the Brothers' tenuous alliance with Gamal Abdel Nasser's regime of pan-Arabic socialism disintegrated into discord and persecution – is the government of Saudi Arabia. The Kingdom, naturally, has long been held in high esteem by the ruling class, portrayed as America's stalwart "ally" against "extremism." Yet the Saudis have poured billions of dollars into the establishment of mosques, madrassas, and Islamic community centers throughout the West. Operating under the stewardship of Brotherhood satellites and allies, this transnational network strives not merely to carve out a place for Islam at our ecumenical table but radically to transform the West. "It is the nature of Islam to dominate, not to be dominated," Banna taught. The mission of Islam is "to impose its law on all nations and to extend its power to the entire planet."

A prime target of Brotherhood attentions has been the United States. For three generations, starting in the early '60s with the founding of the Muslim Students Association (MSA), which now boasts hundreds of chapters in American universities, the Brotherhood has raised a formidable Islamist infrastructure. It is composed of thousands of operatives, the nation's best-known Muslim advocacy organizations, and Islamic centers that form what the Brotherhood calls the "axis" of its movement in cities throughout the nation. Under the auspices of the North American Islamic Trust (formed to acquire real estate) and the Islamic Society of North America (formed to continue the MSA's regimen of proselytism), the movement substantially controls about three-quarters of America's 2,300-plus mosques.

The movement's mission is crystal clear, at least to anyone willing simply to listen to what Islamists say. As Sheikh Qaradawi boldly promises, Muslims intend to "conquer America" and "conquer Europe."

The Brothers have always supported violence. It is no surprise that many in their ranks have gone on to found some of the world's most notorious jihadist networks. Still, despite their mixed bloodlines and common goal of installing sharia as the means to establish a global caliphate, the Brotherhood differs sharply from the likes of al Qaeda in its methods and sophistication. Bin Laden's network is a comparatively crude, impulsive, top-down operation that extorts by sheer force and bridles at the very thought of negotiating with its enemies. The Brotherhood is a patient, thoroughgoing, bottom-up movement whose plan unfolds in stages, content to bore into and co-opt the institutions – especially the political, legal, and educational systems – of the societies it targets.

As Banna explained, the first stage involves "propaganda, communication, and information." Controlling the classroom – "pedagogy as propaganda" – is thus seen as the surest way to "recruit and indoctrinate core activists,"

The Muslim Brotherhood considers itself to be engaged in a "civilizational jihad" against the West.

---

explains Islamism expert Steven Emerson. The template has not changed from the Brotherhood's earliest days: establish press outlets to spread the Islamist message and refute its adversaries, and train lecturers to carry its doctrines into schools, mosques, meeting halls, and the media.

In the second stage, the Brothers "endear themselves to the population by creating charities, clinics, schools, and other services." Concurrently, there is attention to military preparedness: formation into "rovers," "battalions," and a "secret apparatus" to spearhead the eventual revolution. This holistic indoctrination would anneal the Brothers for the final stage, "execution." This is the point at which the Muslim communities, having formed countless "battalions" that were fully prepared intellectually, physically, and spiritually, would "conquer . . . every obstinate tyrant."

Brotherhood theory thus recognizes that violence is certain to be necessary; without it, there would be no "Islamic world" to speak of. The use of force, moreover, is a duty when

Muslim land is occupied or cultivated by non-Muslims: Just as sharia regards an individual as a Muslim forever once he has accepted Islam (and thus brutally punishes apostasy), so too does it hold that territory, if any inch of it has ever been under Muslim control, belongs forever to Islam and must be reclaimed by any means necessary if it is lost. It is not for nothing that Islamists refer to Spain as "al-Andalus" and produce maps of "Palestine" in which Israel is conspicuous only by its absence. Nevertheless, violence is considered counter-productive, and hence is discouraged, if it is premature – if it is initiated at a point when Muslims are incapable of securing military victory. Under such circumstances, resort to force is more likely to provoke an enemy response that harms Muslims and rolls back whatever gains they have theretofore made.

Besides, Islamists are fully capable of making great strides in their sharia agenda without violence – or, at least, by opportunistically exploiting the atmosphere of intimidation created by terrorist violence. This is why, when Sheikh Qaradawi exclaims that Islam will "conquer" America and Europe, he is quick to add that this will be done not by the sword but by *dawa*. This is the proselytism of Islam by nonviolent (or, to be more accurate, previolent) means, such as infiltration of our law and our education system. Robert Spencer, director of the indispensable *Jihad Watch* website, has appropriately labeled this phenomenon "stealth jihad." Another good term for it is "sabotage."

"Sabotage" is not my term. It is the very word used by the Muslim Brotherhood itself. Several years ago, the FBI seized from the home of a top Ikhwan operative in the U.S. an internal 1991 memo written by Mohamed Akram, a Qaradawi confederate and, at that time, the Brotherhood's American leader. Titled "An Explanatory Memorandum on the General Strategic Goal for the Group in North America," the document was directed to the Brotherhood's global leadership and outlined its American strategy:

The Ikhwan must understand that their work in America is a kind of grand Jihad in eliminating and destroying the Western civilization from within and "sabotaging" its miserable house by their hands and the hands of the believers so that it is eliminated and God's religion is made victorious over all other religions.

The memo elaborated that the Islamic "movement," led by the Brotherhood, would proceed with its "settlement process" in the U.S. This process was seen as critical to carrying out what Akram described as a "civilization jihad" – boring sharia standards into American society, hollowing out the West from within.

While the memo is blunt and thus startling, it is hardly singular. It tracks 80 years of Brotherhood theory and a mainstream construction of Islam that dates back centuries. It also echoes a 12-point plan to "establish an Islamic government on earth" that was set forth in an earlier memo seized from an Ikhwan redoubt in Switzerland after the 9/11 attacks. As Brotherhood analyst Patrick Poole recounts, that document, called "The Project," outlines:

a flexible, multi-phased, long-term approach to the "cultural invasion" of the West. Calling for the utilization of various tactics, ranging from immigration, infiltration, surveillance, propaganda, protest, deception, political legitimacy and terrorism, The Project has served for more than two decades as the Muslim Brotherhood "master plan." . . . Rather than focusing on terrorism as the sole method of group action, as is the case with Al-Qaeda, in perfect postmodern fashion the use of terror falls into a multiplicity of options available to progressively infiltrate, confront, and eventually establish Islamic domination over the West.

Key to the accomplishment of this agenda is the creation of autonomous Muslim enclaves – parallel societies adherent to sharia. It is a strategy analysts have aptly labeled "voluntary apartheid." That it is a Trojan horse cannot be seriously doubted. Qaradawi is candid: "Were we to convince Western leaders and decision-makers of our right to live according to our faith – ideologically, legislatively, and ethically – without imposing our views or inflicting harm upon them, we would have traversed an immense barrier in our quest for an Islamic state."

Notice, again, the mindset: *without inflicting harm upon them.* While it should be difficult to fathom anything more harmful to individual liberty than the establishment of an Islamic state, Qaradawi adroitly reads the West's temperament: tunnel-focused on terrorism, concerned only about forcible damage to life, limb, and property. As long as we're told there will be no *harm,* he rightly figures we'll assume he means no *terrorism.* If terrorism is not in the equation, we go back to sleep – back to broadly accommodating people who tell us, flat-out, that their goal is our elimination.

The enclave strategy has already been implemented to great effect in Europe. Qara-dawi made it sound unthreatening enough. In early 2005, he encouraged the continent's swelling Muslim population to integrate into

European society. There was just one caveat: The integration must be done "without violating the rules of sharia." There is only one way such an integration can happen on Qaradawi's terms: Muslims must capitalize on their unity and growing strength to pressure

---

Muslim Brotherhood theory recognizes that violence is certain to be necessary; without it, there would be no "Islamic world" to speak of.

Europe into adopting sharia, bit by bit.

Obviously, the strategy is working. The eminent Bernard Lewis stunned Western readers when he recently predicted that Europe will be Islamic by the end of the 21st century. The truth is, he may be several decades behind the curve. Already, the European and

Australian landscapes are dotted by "no-go" zones: Muslim neighborhoods where police no longer patrol, sovereignty having been effectively surrendered to the local imams and Muslim gangs. In France, for example, police estimate that some 8 million people (12 percent of the population – and climbing) live in the country's 751 *zones urbaines sensibles*, sensitive urban areas.

To this point, the United States has not succumbed to the physical takeover of territory. Nevertheless, Islamists have a knack for finding the weak links in every society. In America, those links are our law and our conceit that multiculturalism is an unassailable value – even to the extent of surrendering our core principles to accommodate cultural supremacists.

The Detroit suburb of Dearborn has one of the nation's heaviest concentrations of Muslim immigrants. It is a hotbed of Brother - hood activity and support for Hamas and Hezbollah. In June, four Christian missionaries were arrested by uniformed police outside an Arab festival. They were accused of disturbing the peace. Their crime? They were handing out copies of St. John's Gospel on a public street. One of the missionaries managed to videotape the goings-on, at least until his camera was seized. Plainly, they were not engaged in a form of incitement or public commotion – not in the United States, a pluralistic society in which the distribution of even offensive materials enjoys constitutional protection. What the missionaries were violating was sharia – specifically, its prohibition against preaching religions other than Islam.

To be sure, the police probably did not see themselves as enforcing sharia. They were trying to prevent the provocation of Muslims, who seem preternaturally prone to overheated – and worse – responses to the types of occasionally displeasing stimuli people in the West are expected to tolerate for the greater good of living in a free and well-informed society. But it is irrelevant what the police and policymakers subjectively think – irrelevant what their good intentions may be – if the effect of their actions is to enforce a theocratic code.

This is the state of play in modern America. In 2009, Jytte Klausen wrote a scholarly book on the 2005 Muslim riots over a Dutch newspaper's publication of cartoon caricatures of the prophet Muhammad. Yale University Press refused to publish it until Klausen agreed to censor not only photographs of the cartoons but such classical representations of Muhammad as Gustave Doré's illustration for Canto 28 (the "sowers of religious discord") of Dante's *Inferno*. The cartoon controversy itself drew stinging State Department rebuke – for the newspaper, which was said to have exhibited intolerable insensitivity.

A cartoonist named Molly Norris was recently forced to change her name and go underground for suggesting – in a show of solidarity – an "Everybody Draw Mohammed Day." The government could not protect her; reports indicate that she flew the coop on the advice of the FBI. Her former employer, the *Seattle Weekly*, could manage nothing more than a meek announcement that "there is no more Molly." Media cowardice is now rote when it comes to Islam. Thus did *The Washington Post* spike a "Where's Muhammad?" spoof in which the prophet nowhere appeared — and, by this craven act, validate cartoonist Wiley Miller's point about Western timidity. Comedy Central similarly purged from an episode of its popular series "South Park" all references to Muhammad. An Islamic website had threatened retaliation.

Nor is free speech the only American principle wilting under sharia pressure. In New Jersey, a Muslim woman was serially raped by her Muslim husband (who was about to divorce her). Yet a state judge refused to issue a protective order based on sexual assault. The evidence showed the man had told the crying woman, "This is according to our religion. You are my wife; I can do anything to you. The woman, she should submit and do anything I ask her to do." Under sharia principles, a wife may not refuse her husband's requests for sex. Accordingly, the judge reasoned – if we may call it that – that the man should not be punished because "he was operating under his belief" that his religion countenanced "his practices."

Fortunately, the New Jersey case was reversed on appeal. The higher court held that at least in this instance, "religious precepts" should not trump the criminal law. It is worth bearing in mind, however, that many outrageous decisions by courts of first instance never get appealed. We are aware of this case only because the ruling was challenged. We do not know the extent of sharia encroachment in cases that don't get appealed – or never make it to court in the first place. We know only that the more sharia is legitimized in our law, the less inclination there will be to contest it, resulting in still further encroachment.

In Minnesota, for example, there has been a dramatic influx of Muslim immigration, especially from Somalia. Sharia, consequently, is enjoying boom times. The state was the first to elect a Muslim member of Congress. Keith Ellison, a hard Left apologist for Louis Farrakhan and Symbionese Liberation Army radicals, a recipient of enthusiastic support from such Muslim Brotherhood tentacles as the Council on American-Islamic Relations (CAIR), and a public sympathizer of convicted

---

The more sharia is legitimized in our law, the less inclination there will be to contest it, resulting in still further encroachment.

Palestinian Islamic Jihad operative Sami al-Arian, took the oath of office by swearing on the Koran.

Meantime, at the airport in Minneapolis, Muslim taxi drivers routinely refuse to ferry passengers suspected of carrying alcohol, which is prohibited by sharia. Following a now-typical pattern, rather than yanking licenses, the state authority sought advice from the local chapter of the Muslim American Society (the Brotherhood's semiofficial presence in the U.S.) and then sought to reason with the cabbies, suggesting that sharia be construed as barring the *drinking* of alcohol, not its transportation. Quite apart from whether this is true (and it is at best debatable), this resolution implicitly conceded the premise that sharia was relevant to the dispute's resolution. Concurrently, it enhanced the prestige of the Brotherhood's network.

A Minnesota college student and the dog he uses for medical assistance were threatened by Muslim students at a high school where he was doing required field work. Under sharia, canines are considered unclean. True to form, the college, unwilling to confront the Islamic aggression, resolved the incident by waiving the field work. An official sputtered that while protecting disabled students was important, the regrettable incident was "part of the growth process when we become more diverse." The state is becoming very diverse indeed. A charter school, named Tarek ibn Ziyad Academy after the Muslim general who conquered Spain in the eighth century, has operated for years with taxpayer funds under Muslim American Society auspices. At its 2007 convention, the MAS featured the school in a brochure under the heading "Establishing Islam in Minnesota." The state also uses public funding to facilitate Muslim mortgages, in compliance with sharia's proscription against interest payments.

While these developments are worrisome, thus far they have largely been confined to locales with high concentrations of Muslims – few and far between in a country of 300 million, where Muslims account for about 1 percent of the population. Much more alarming is the Obama administration's embrace of the sharia agenda. That portends accommodations at the national level, affecting the rights of every American.

The trouble started in Cairo. In preparation for the president's 2009 al-Azhar speech, the Obama administration invited members of the Muslim Brotherhood to attend. Put aside that the Brotherhood is a banned organization in Egypt – Ikhwan operatives murdered President Sadat in 1981 – and thus that the administration's overture needlessly ruffled the authoritarian Mubarak regime's feathers. At the time Obama spoke, the Brotherhood had been identified as the hub of the most significant terrorism-financing case ever undertaken by the Justice Department, the prosecution of an ostensible Islamic "charity," the Holy Land Foundation for Relief and Development (HLF), for pouring millions into the coffers of Hamas. The Brotherhood was not only at the center of the enterprise, having set up HLF as a jihadist piggy bank. The Brotherhood's principal American arms – CAIR, the Islamic Society of North America (ISNA), and the North American Islamic Trust, to name just three of many – were also cited by the Justice Department as unindicted coconspirators and shown by prosecutors to have advanced the scheme in material ways.

The Obama administration has nevertheless provided these and other Islamist entities with an open door. In fact, despite ISNA's history of collaborating in the financing of Hamas, the administration dispatched Valerie Jarrett, the president's confidant and top political adviser, to deliver the keynote address at ISNA's annual convention. Meantime, at al-Azhar, while sketching a staggering revisionist history of Islam's interactions with America, the West, and Israel, Obama committed to ease what he limned as American restrictions on *zakat*, the Islamic requirement of charitable giving (to Muslims only, of course). But there are no such restrictions. Our law prohibits only material support to terrorist organizations. Muslims have been prosecuted under it not because they are Muslims but because funds have found their way to violent jihadists.

Equally troubling is the administration's promotion of sharia in our financial system. This thriving field, called sharia-compliant finance (SCF), is the mid-20th-century brainchild of the Islamist intellectual Abu-Ala Maududi, whose goals, as Daniel Pipes summarizes, were "to minimize relations with non-Muslims, strengthen the collective sense of Muslim identity, extend Islam into a new area of human activity, and modernize without Westernizing." Sheikh Qaradawi refers to this aspect of the Brotherhood's civilizational battle as "financial jihad" – co-opting the financial system to serve Islamist goals, such as Hamas's war to destroy Israel.

With the government takeover of the American International Group (AIG), American taxpayers became the owners of the world's most lavishly funded provider of sharia-compliant insurance products – operated by the U.S. Treasury Department. Like other companies that participate in SCF, AIG retains an advisory board of sharia experts. Such boards often include Islamist ideologues. They tell companies which investments are permissible (halal) and which are not (haram). AIG's "Sharia Supervisory Committee" includes a Pakistani named Imran Ashraf

Usmani, who is the son and student of Taqi Usmani, a globally renowned sharia authority who has written that Muslims in the West must engage in jihad against the countries in which they live.

In the insurance business, those who purchase policies pay premiums, which insurers like AIG then invest. To be sharia-compliant, investments must not be made in enterprises Islam forbids, e.g., finance (because it makes money off interest), pork, gambling, and alcohol. Sounds harmless enough . . . except forbidden enterprises would also include businesses that support or otherwise work with the U.S. armed forces. Islamists consider our military to be an "infidel force" that is "at war with Islam."

SCF requires that investments be constantly monitored and that any interest payments be purged. This is done by skimming off a percentage that is then channeled – at the direction of the advisory board – to an Islamic "charity." Of course, as no one knows better than the Treasury Department, many

> *The Obama administration has provided Islamist entities with an open door.*

such charities are merely fronts for the financing of terrorist organizations. This is not an accident. When Sheikh Qaradawi speaks of "financial jihad" as an Islamic obligation, he's not kidding. In Islamist ideology, funding those who "fight in Allah's cause" – e.g., Hamas – is one of the eight categories of permissible *zakat*, the aforementioned Muslim obligation of charitable giving. So an American company that practices SCF is, wittingly or not, advancing the jihadist agenda: It will deny financing to enterprises that help our military combat terrorists while running the risk that its sharia advisers will steer funding to those same terrorists. Nevertheless, the Treasury Department is currently fighting lawsuits that seek to get the government out of the SCF business.

The most harrowing aspect of Obama's "New Beginning" has been his cultivation of the Organization of the Islamic Conference (OIC). This 57-government enterprise (56 nations plus the Palestinian Authority) is the largest voting bloc in the United Nations. It is pervasively influenced by Brotherhood ideologues (as well as by influential Shiite authorities), and its primary mission is to spread sharia globally. Indeed, in 1990, it promulgated the "Cairo Declaration," also known as the "Universal Declaration of Human Rights in Islam," the OIC's answer to the Universal Declaration of Human Rights adopted by the nascent U.N. General Assembly in the aftermath of World War II. The Cairo Declaration "reaffirm[s] the civilizing and historic role of the Islamic Ummah which Allah made the best nation," transparently rejects freedom of conscience (among other liberties), and demands that there be "no crime or punishment except as provided for in the Sharia."

In light of the OIC's evident hostility to the West, the U.S. kept it at arm's length for more than 30 years until the Bush administration, in its waning months, imprudently appointed a special envoy to promote "dialogue" with it. As is its wont, the Obama administration has seized on its predecessor's misstep and inflated it into a looming disaster.

President Obama began his term with a personal invitation to the OIC's secretary-general, encouraging him to visit the White House and explore ways the U.S. and the Islamist bloc can work together. Then he appointed his own OIC special envoy, Rashad Hussain, a 32-year old "*hafiz* of the Koran," as Obama proudly described him (meaning one who has memorized scripture in the original Arabic). Hussain's previous claim to fame – besides helping write Obama's Cairo speech – was an appearance, while at Yale Law School, at a Muslim Students Association conference. There, in short order, he managed to decry the Patriot Act, blast the Sami al-Arian terrorism indictment as a "travesty of justice" (al-Arian later pleaded guilty), and berate the Justice Department's similar "persecution" of other convicted terrorists.

Finally, in May 2009, President Obama joined with the OIC as a cosponsor (with Egypt) of a United Nations resolution that condemns "negative stereotyping of religions." The resolution exhorts all nations to take "effective measures" to "address and combat" incidents involving "any advocacy of . . . religious hatred" that could be construed as "incitement" – not just to "violence," but to any form of "discrimination," or even to mere "hostility." The measure would rely on international law to install sharia's ban on speech that is critical of Islam.

In sum, the ethos of intimidation that already muzzles examination of Islam – its law, its culture, and the activities of Islamists – could soon be backed by the coercive power of law. And while this is precisely the type of abuse the First Amendment is designed to prevent, the Constitution could prove unavailing. There is already a five-justice majority on the Supreme Court that favors resorting to international and foreign law in the interpretation of constitutional provisions. Moreover, Justice Elena Kagan, Obama's second appointee to the high court – who, as dean of Harvard Law School, promoted the university's Saudi-funded sharia studies programs – belittled the value of free speech as an academic. She argued, as Obama's solicitor-general, that "categories of speech" may be suppressed when the government decides the "societal costs" of permitting them are too high.

It is commonplace to snicker at the thought that America could be "conquered" by Islam. And if we were talking about conquest by al Qaeda or some invading jihadist army, derision would be a justifiable response. But our challenge is sabotage from within: a civilization no longer sure its values are worth defending, steadily abraded by a civilization certain that Allah intends for it to prevail. As we snicker, we might bear in mind that they used to snicker in Europe, too.

First American edition published in 2010 by Encounter Books,
an activity of Encounter for Culture and Education, Inc.,
a nonprofit, tax exempt corporation.
Encounter Books website address: www.encounterbooks.com

Manufactured in the United States and printed on
acid-free paper. The paper used in this publication meets
the minimum requirements of ANSI/NISO z39.48–1992
(R 1997) (*Permanence of Paper*).

FIRST AMERICAN EDITION

LIBRARY OF CONGRESS CATALOGING-IN-PUBLICATION DATA

McCarthy, Andrew C.
How Obama embraces Islam's Sharia agenda / by Andrew C.
McCarthy.
p.   cm. — (Encounter broadsides)
ISBN-13: 978-1-59403-558-6 (pbk. : alk. paper)
ISBN-10: 1-59403-558-x (pbk. : alk. paper)
1. United States—Foreign relations—2009– 2. Obama, Barack.
3. United States—Foreign relations—Islamic countries. 4. Islamic
countries—Foreign relations—United States. 5. Islamic law.
6. Terrorism—Government policy—United States. I. Title.
E907.M33 2010
327.7309767—dc22
2010044430

10 9 8 7 6 5 4 3 2 1

SERIES DESIGN BY CARL W. SCARBROUGH